The Azte

Tony D. Triggs

Published by Collins
An imprint of HarperCollinsPublishers
The News Building
1 London Bridge Street
London
SE1 9GF

Browse the complete Collins catalogue at
www.collinseducation.com

First published in 2006 by Folens Limited, as part of the *Folens Primary History* series.
Reprinted 2008. Previously published as *A Time to Remember: The Aztecs*.

10 9 8 7

ISBN: 978-0-00-746399-2

British Library Cataloguing in Publication Data
A catalogue record for this publication is available from the British Library.

Acknowledgements
The author and publisher wish to thank the following for permission to use copyright material:
Neg. No. 329247. Courtesy of the Department of Library Services, American Museum of Natural History, p38
Ancient Art and Architecture Collection/Ronald Sheridan, pp4, 5, 26, 37, 40-41, 45, 57, 62-63
The Trustees of the British Museum, pp19, 22, 32, 33, 34-35, 36, 37, 39, 43, 44, 48, 49, 55, 56
C. M. Dixon Colour Photo Library, pp43, 57
Mary Evans Picture Library, pp12, 38
Michael Holford, pp6, 10-11, 33, 52, 57
Natural History Photographic Agency, pp16 (Ivan Polunin), 17 (G. I. Bernard),
18 (Stephen Dalton and Carl Switak), 60 (Douglas Dickens)
National Maritime Museum, p5
The Board of Trustees of the Royal Armouries, pp62-63
Royal Geographical Society, p7
The Wellcome Trust, p58, 59

Every effort has been made to trace copyright holders and to obtain their permission for the use of copyright material. The author and publisher will gladly receive any information enabling them to rectify any error or omission in subsequent editions.

Editors: Saskia Gwinn and Joanne Mitchell
Layout artist: Suzanne Ward
Illustrations: Peter Dennis of Linda Rogers Associates, Tony Randell of Tony Randell Illustration
Cover design: Blayney Partnership
Cover image: Charles Lenars/CORBIS

Printed and bound by CPI Group (UK) Ltd, Croydon, CR0 4YY

Contents

Source A *Christopher Columbus' ship, the Santa Maria.*

It was the summer of 1492, and the streets of a little Spanish port were unusually busy. A Genoese sea captain called Christopher Columbus was preparing three ships for a dangerous journey. There were carpenters finishing off the ships, merchants bringing food, candles and other supplies and 100 sailors shouting noisily. Led by Columbus, they were planning to sail westwards across the stormy Atlantic Ocean.

No one knew what they would find, for the ocean had not been properly explored. Some people thought the Earth was flat and that the ships and men would probably disappear over a huge waterfall at its edge.

Source B
An astrolabe, used for showing the positions of the sun and stars.

The shape of the Earth was a very important question. Only land to the east of Europe had been explored. Spices and other goods from Asia had to be brought to Spain by a long and difficult route. Spices, grown in islands known as the Indies, were shipped to the Asian mainland and then carried overland to the west coast of India. From here they were shipped to Egypt, and on to Spain (and the rest of western Europe) by sea or land.

A globe. Some people previously thought the Earth was flat.

Merchants who brought the spices from the east faced many dangers. They were sometimes killed by disease or bandits, or their ships sank in storms at sea. These difficulties meant spices were very expensive.

Nowadays, we can do without spice, but in those days it was very important. Farmers knew that in winter there would not be enough grass to feed their cattle, sheep and pigs, so they killed a lot of them in the autumn. People preserved the meat with salt or spice, for eating during the winter.

Source C *Christopher Columbus 1451–1506.*

At sea with Columbus

1. How do people preserve food today?
2. Why was spice more important in Columbus' time than it is today?
3. Looking at **Source A**, list the differences between the Santa Maria and a modern ocean-going ship.
4. Look at **Source B**. Why was an astrolabe necessary?
5. List six words to describe Christopher Columbus (as seen in **Source C**).

Key ideas

astrolabe	preserving food
merchant shipping	trade
navigation	

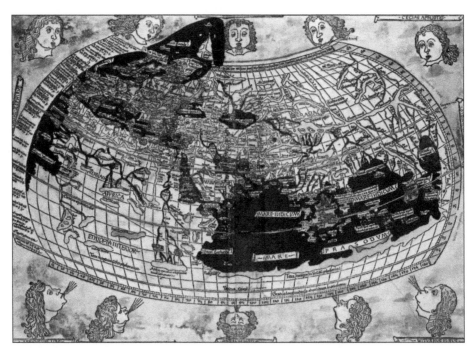

Source D *A map of the world from 1486.*

Like most educated people, Columbus thought that the Earth was round like a ball. If this was true, there had to be two different ways to go round it. Merchants from Spain were heading east to get to the Indies, but what if they went the other way? Columbus believed that if they did this they would get to the Indies by an easier route. He wanted to be the first to find this route and he was willing to risk his life at sea in order to do so.

Columbus was right about the Earth being round. But Columbus was also wrong about something. He did not know that North, Central and South America blocked his sea route to the Indies. When he made his voyage he landed on islands off the coast of Central America.

He thought he had reached the Indies and he never found out his mistake. Columbus had found the Americas – a whole New World that people in Europe had never heard of. When they realised the truth they began to call the Indies the East Indies. The islands that Columbus had discovered were known as the West Indies.

Mapping the world

1. Look at **Source D**. Think about when this map was made. Which parts of the world are missing? Why?
2. The map in **Source E** was made after Columbus had reached the Americas. Compare it with a world map today. Are there any differences? (Look carefully at the shape of South America.)
3. Use the map in **Source E** to pick out the journey the spice merchants made in Columbus' time. (Be sure you know where the East Indies are before you begin.)
4. Pretend that you are a merchant living in the 16th century. Use the map in **Source E**. Now use an atlas to help you to plan a new route for bringing spice from the East Indies to Europe.

Key ideas

invasion   ruler
merchant shipping

It is often hard to say why something happened exactly when it did. The timing of Columbus' voyage is linked to something that happened a few months earlier.

For several centuries, most of Spain and Portugal had been ruled by people called Moors who had come from North Africa. During the 15th century, the Spanish and Portuguese gradually pushed the Moors out of their lands. In 1492 they conquered the last Moorish city, Granada. Almost immediately, the King and Queen of Spain, Ferdinand and Isabella, agreed to help Columbus make his voyage.

Why 1492?

1. Why do you think the Spanish King and Queen felt the time was right to help Columbus make his voyage?
2. Imagine you are a sailor who believes the world is flat. How might you persuade the other sailors to go back?
3. If you were Christopher Columbus, what would you say to the sailors to persuade them to continue?

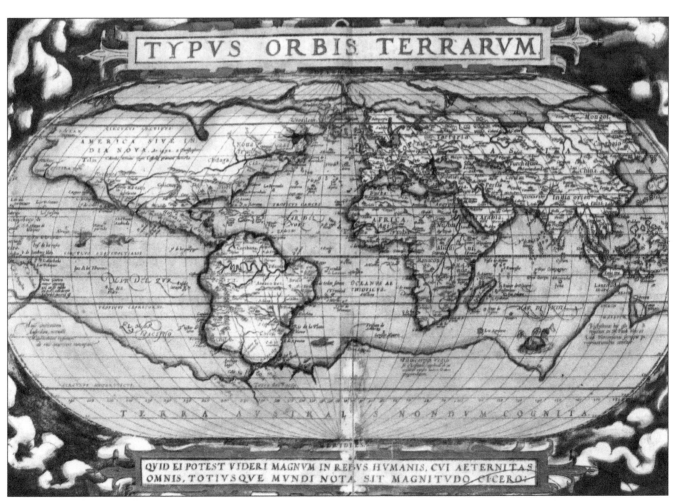

Source E *A world map drawn in 1571.*

Columbus began his voyage of discovery on the 3rd August, 1492. He set sail in the Santa Maria with 50 men. There were two other ships which had about 25 men each.

His ships were not very large, and each was tightly packed with supplies. To sail across oceans never before chartered, in such small ships, was an impressive achievement.

Key

Captain's cabin	☐	Sailmaker	☐
Stores	☐	Galley	☐
Ship's boat	☐	Helmsman	☐
Gun deck	☐	Main deck	☐
Capstan	☐	Wine or water casks	☐
Mast	☐		

A sailor's life

Look at the drawing in **Source A** which is of a ship very similar to Columbus' Santa Maria. Study the key carefully and find out the meaning of any words you do not know.

1. Write the correct number in each box to match the numbers on the drawing.
2. Does the ship seem to be under attack? If not, what do you think the man with the bow and arrow is doing?
3. What do you think the men at A and B are doing?
4. The ship would be equipped with sails before the journey. Why do you think they still took a sailmaker on board?
5. List some of the other people who would be needed on a voyage.
6. Suggest some of the punishments captains might give to men who disobeyed their orders.

Source A

Columbus was away from Spain for nearly a year. He had to make sure that everything he would need was taken on board before he set sail.

Away for a year

Look at **Sources B–E** of things found on the ships.

1. Label the pictures you recognise and describe what they were used for.
2. Listed below are some features of life at sea. Try to add two extra ones in the spaces. Put ticks in the boxes beside the good features and put crosses in the boxes beside the bad features.

Often wet and cold ☐

Chance of getting rich ☐

Lots of adventure ☐

Maggots in food ☐

Poor diet, leading to gum disease and loss of teeth ☐

Few pastimes ☐

Gambling (betting) games ☐

Harsh punishments ☐

Chance of going somewhere hot ☐

Rats, lice and fleas ☐

Sailors often thugs and criminals ☐

Work at all hours ☐

High risk of danger and death ☐

Not much sleep ☐

Men only – no wives or children on board ☐

Storms and seasickness ☐

_____ ☐

_____ ☐

3. Count up the number of ticks and crosses you have. Decide if you would have liked to have been a sailor.

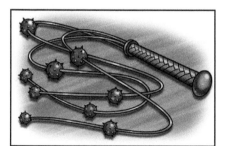

Source B

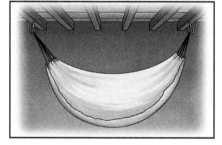

Source C

Source D

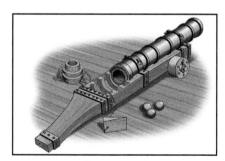

Source E

Asked to sail the world

Captains sometimes found it difficult to get a full crew.

Write a short conversation in which a captain asks you to join his ship. Are you keen to go or are you frightened? Perhaps he thinks the Earth is round but you think it's flat. You can use the list of good and bad points to give you extra ideas. Perhaps you could act out the conversation for your class.

Columbus was followed by other Spaniards. Columbus had wanted to find things out, but these people wanted to seize new lands for the Spanish King and Queen. Land, gold and other riches would make Spain powerful and wealthy.

The captains and sailors knew that the King would reward them well. Often he let them keep much of the gold and land for themselves. This meant that they could set up farms and use the local people as slaves.

Key ideas

Christianity	crusading
conquering	power
conversion	religion
cross	slavery

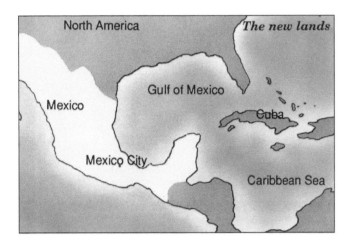

Source A *A drawing from the time showing natives fleeing from the Spaniards.*

By the start of the 16th century the Spaniards were ruling Cuba, Haiti and other islands in the West Indies. The Spaniards made the natives give up their gods and turn to Christianity. This was the Spaniards' own religion, and they felt that they should fight to make others believe it too. They sometimes called themselves 'Soldiers of Christ'. They were not just being greedy for land and gold: they were doing what they thought God wanted.

In 1519, a Spaniard called Hernán Cortés sailed from Cuba to Yucatán (now part of Mexico). He waved a special flag as he went on board his ship. The words were in Latin (the language people in Europe used for reading and writing).

The sign of the cross

Look at the picture of Cortés' flag (**Source A**).

1. What were the Spaniards' two main aims when they sailed to new countries?
2. The cross was a sort of badge for the Spaniards' religion. What was their religion called?
3. Discuss the meaning of Cortés' flag. Think of another way of saying the same thing. You could draw a flag and put your own words on it.
4. Look at **Source A** again. Describe how the natives are fleeing from the Spaniards.

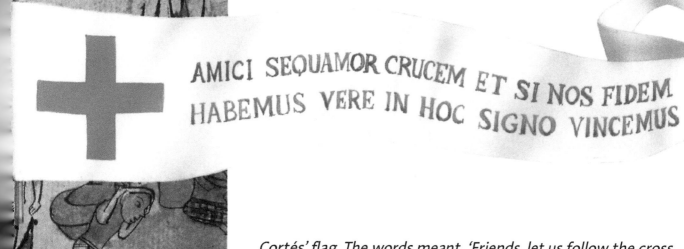

Cortés' flag. The words meant, 'Friends, let us follow the cross, and if we have faith we will surely conquer in this sign'.

Source B *Hernán Cortés 1485–1547.*

Andrés de Tapia sailed to Mexico with Cortés in 1519. He wrote about what they found when they reached a small island.

This island had about 2000 natives … who worshipped idols and killed animals to make the idols happy. One of the idols was in a high tower at the edge of the sea. The idol was made of baked clay and was hollow inside. It was fixed against a wall, and it looked as if someone could go round the back and get inside through a secret entrance … The Indians said that the idol spoke.

At the foot of the tower the natives offered quail (a bird) and the blood of quail, and they burnt the sap of special trees to make a sweet smell.

They said they did this when they needed rain, and that rain always fell soon afterwards.

Cortés called all the natives together. He begged them to tear down their idols, and they seemed to do so willingly. Then he had (Christian) crosses put up all over the island, and at the tower.

Key ideas

Christianity	idol
conversion	worship
cross	

Cortés Follows the Cross

Cortés did not speak the natives' language, but one of the Spaniards knew it well. This Spaniard had joined Cortés' men when they arrived at the island. He explained that he and some other Spaniards had been shipwrecked there about 10 years earlier. One of his shipmates was married to a native, but the rest had died. The married Spaniard refused to join Cortés, pointing out that his ears were pierced and his hands and face were tattooed.

Source C

The Aztecs were the main tribe in Mexico. Above and below you can see two of the figures they made and worshipped.

Aztec religion

Look at the pictures of the idols made by the Aztecs (**Sources C** and **D**), and think about what Tapia wrote.

1. Choose words from the box below to describe the gods that the idols represent.

   | kind | fierce | cruel |
   | gentle | powerful | |

   Explain why you have chosen each word.
2. Why did Cortés want the natives to destroy their idols?
3. Did they destroy their idols? How do you know?

Source D

Dress and decoration

Imagine you are the Spaniard with pierced ears and tattoos.

1. Describe what would happen if you went back to Spain.
2. Compare the picture of Cortés (**Source B**) with a modern sailor. List the similarities and differences.
3. Is the picture likely to show Cortés as he really was? Explain your answer.

Life as a native

Pretend that you are one of the natives.

Write your own account of how the Spaniards treated your gods. Use Tapia's report to help you. Your work might start like this: 'About 2000 of us live on the island. We worship our gods by giving them some of our favourite food ...'

Tapia's Chronicle

From the *Chronicle of Andrés de Tapia* who travelled with Cortés.

A storm hit and set the ships adrift, but by following the course he (Cortés) had given them they met at a small island in the sea near the mainland, which the natives call Auçamil. Of all the ships there was only one missing ...

This island has about two thousand people, and is some five leagues from end to end, and one and a half or two leagues across. Its people worshipped idols to which they made sacrifices, especially to one that was on a high tower at the edge of the sea. This idol was made of baked clay and was hollow, set with lime against a wall with a secret entrance behind it, where it looked as though a man could enter and invest himself in the idol. This must have been so, because as we later understood it the Indians said that the idol spoke. We found in front of the idol, at the foot of the tower, a cross made of lime that was an estado and a half high with a merloned stone wall, where the Indians said they offered quail and the blood of quail, and burned a resin in the manner of incense. They said they did this when they needed rain, whereupon it would rain ...

After leaving the island the marqués (Cortés) sailed his armada somewhat close to the mainland, in search of the missing ship, and by following the course he had set (for the voyage from Cuba) he found the ship in a cove. Strung along her rigging she had a large number of hare and rabbit skins, and some deer hides both large and small. The Spaniards of this ship said that when they arrived they saw a Spanish dog running on the shore and barking at the ship. The captain and some of the men landed and saw it was a greyhound bitch of good size. She came up and greeted them happily, then returned to the woods and began bringing them rabbits. They hunted with her during the time they were there and had prepared a supply of jerked rabbit and deer meat.

From here the marqués sailed to the point he called De Las Mujeres, because all the idols that were there on some salt flats were fashioned like women, and he was there two days waiting for the weather to clear. While on my ship I saw some of the men catch a fish they call a tiburón, which is a kind of shark. It turned out that this fish had eaten all the men's meat rations, which were salt pork and had been tied to lines over the sides of the ships and left to soak. We caught the shark with a hook and some lines drawn through the eye of the hook, but could not use the tackle to raise it without listing the ship, so we killed it in the water, from the skiff, and hauled it on board in pieces. Inside its body were more than thirty sides of pork, a cheese, two or three shoes, and a tin plate. The plate appeared to have fallen overboard with the cheese from the ship commanded by Pedro de Alvarado, whom the marqués had made captain of one of the ships of his armada. There were thirteen ships, and the men in all the armada numbered about five hundred and sixty. The largest of the ships was a hundred tons, and three were of sixty to eighty tons, while the rest were smaller. As for the meat that was taken out of the fish, we ate it because it was more unsalted than the other and tasted better.

From here the fleet sailed to a river that runs through the province of Tabasco. He left the larger ships out at sea and put the men and artillery in the smallest skiffs, with which he started up the river. He was intercepted by certain Indian warriors, and talked to them through the interpreter, promising not to take anything of theirs nor allow any harm to come to them if they received him in peace and listened to the reasons for his being there. They asked for a day's leave to give their reply, and the marqués waited with the men and skiffs on a tiny islet formed by the river.

As it turned out, they had asked for deferment in order to take out their belongings. The next day about ten o'clock the marqués took his men in the boats towards land. The Indians were arrayed for war with their bows and arrows and spears, and began shooting toward the boats. The marqués demanded several times to be received in peace, adding that he begged them insistently because he knew they would otherwise be destroyed; but they refused, and threatened to kill us if we came ashore. And so we landed and their town was taken, and the marqués and his men took quarters in a courtyard where there were rooms used by the people who served the idols.

Upon retiring that night he placed guards in the camp, and in the morning sent three patrols out on some wide roads leading in from villages, to look for fruits and things like plants to eat. The patrols followed the roads as far as some tilled fields belonging to the townspeople. There they encountered some Indians who fought with them, and they brought a few back. At camp these Indians told us how they were gathering to give us battle and fight with all their might to kill and then eat us.

Food and Drink

Source A *A modern photograph of cocoa pods.*

In one place, the natives gave them cooked turkey; in another they gave them fruit and maize.

Tapia tells an interesting story which shows us what the Spaniards usually ate on board their ships:

We caught a shark with a hook and some ropes, but we could not haul it up because the ship would have tipped over, so we got in a skiff (small boat) and killed it in the water; then we cut it up and hauled it aboard in pieces. It turned out that the shark had eaten all the men's meat rations which had been tied to lines and left over the sides of the ship to soak. Inside the shark we found more than 30 sides of pork, a cheese, two or three shoes and a tin plate. The plate must have fallen overboard with the cheese. Although it had been in the shark's stomach we ate the pork because it tasted less salty than usual.

Cortés sailed right round the coast of Yucatán and landed where the city of Veracruz now stands. At that time, there was a native village on the shore. The villagers did not seem to have much treasure, but they had all kinds of food the Spaniards had not seen before. The natives gave the Spaniards food as a way of being friendly.

The men must have eaten the shark as well as the pork from inside it. Fresh fish was a treat. Most of their food was dry, hard and stale, or salty to prevent it from going bad in the hot weather.

A present-day artist's view of the scene during Tapia's voyage when the sailors cut open the shark.

Maize was one of the Aztecs' most important crops, but the Spaniards had never heard of it. The seeds are the edible part of the plant. When the Spaniards saw them they thought they were little peas.

The natives sent the Spaniards 20 slaves, who showed them how to grind the seeds into flour between stones. They added water and shaped the dough into little flat cakes. These were baked on special flat bricks or steamed in a cooking pot. Roughly ground maize was used to make porridge.

Nowadays, most people eat maize. It is used to make cornflakes and other foods. We also make the little flat cakes the Aztecs used to make. We call them tortillas.

Source B *A modern photograph of maize.*

Food at sea

Read Tapia's story of the food eaten at sea.

1. Why were the sailors soaking their meat?
2. Why did they take salty meat with them?
3. What fresh food could they get at sea?

Look at **Source B** and read the information.

4. Imagine the Spaniards seeing these new crops for the first time. How might they have described them in a letter to friends at home?
5. How did they find out what to do with them?
6. How do you think the sailors felt when the natives gave them food rather than treasure?

Cooking for Cortés

Pretend that you are the cook on board Cortés' ship, anchored just off the coast of Mexico. Tapia tells us that Cortés 'dined heartily', and that he was 'not fussy about his food, but he liked a good meal on special occasions'.

1. Work out a meal for a special occasion which you can make from local foods. (You will have to send someone ashore for supplies.)
2. Design an attractive menu to go on Cortés' table to describe your meal.

Key ideas

cultivating crops   slavery
preserving food

The natives gave the Spaniards vegetables that they had never seen before. One was the sweet potato, which is like an ordinary potato. The Spaniards had never seen any sort of potatoes. They thought the sweet potatoes were like carrots.

One of the sailors, called Díaz, wrote about another new vegetable:

Yucca are grown in mounds of earth and look like turnips. The roots are poisonous and harmful until they are chopped up and cooked in a special way. They can then be scraped, crushed and baked to make a sort of bread.

A yucca plant.

The natives drank a lot of cocoa. They collected the cocoa beans, ground them up and added cold water. Then they beat the mixture with spoons to make it frothy.

A Spaniard described another plant which the natives used to make a drink:

It is a prickly bush that has leaves the thickness of a knee and the length of an arm ... From its centre sprouts a trunk as high as three men and as thick as a child of six or seven. At a certain time each year ... they bore a hole at the bottom and get the juice ... After a day or two they drink it ... and they do not stop until they fall to the ground drunk and senseless. They consider this a great honour.

They also make wine, vinegar and syrup from it; also men's and women's clothing and shoes, as well as cord, house beams, roof tiles and needles for sewing and stitching up wounds, and many other things.

Favourite drinks

Read the description of the 'prickly bush' and look at **Source C**.

1. What sort of plant was the 'prickly bush'?
2. Why do you think the Spaniards did not use its proper name?
3. The Spanish writer tells us some of the things the natives made from the prickly bush. Which pieces of the plant do you think they were made from?
4. What shows the natives' skill in medicine?

Source C *The 'prickly bush' still grows in South America.*

Tapia's Chronicle

Source D

Key ideas

cultivating crops   gods

This page shows some Aztec pictures explaining what the weather (or the gods) could do to the soil and the maize in different years.

The Aztecs

Look at the Aztecs' pictures.

1. Study **Sources D** and **E**. Each source has two pictures. The figure on the right of each picture is an Aztec god. What do you think the other figure is meant to be? How can you tell?
2. Do you think the Aztecs grew the maize, the yuccas and the 'prickly bushes' themselves, or do you think they found them growing wild? Why do you think so?
3. The Aztecs worried about how the weather would affect their crops. The weather affects the crops we grow in Britain today but it worries us less. Discuss this difference and try to think of some reasons for it.

Source E

The Aztecs put fences round small parts of the lake. They collected buckets of mud and poured it into the fenced areas. The mud became firm but it never dried out and it grew good crops. The water all round the gardens kept the plants moist.

The Aztecs planted their seeds in blocks, not rows. They mixed maize and gourds in a special pattern. If you grow maize and gourds you should put them in a similar pattern. As the plants grow you can try to decide why the Aztecs arranged them in this way.

The Aztecs planted maize and gourds in a special pattern.

Crops for cold climates

If you live in a cold district you can grow chilli peppers indoors following these instructions.

1. Plant the chilli seeds in a large pot in April.
2. Place the pot on a sunny windowsill.
3. Green peppers should be ready in July.
4. What colour do they go if you leave them on the plant?
5. The Aztecs used peppers to flavour their tortillas. What do they taste like?

Sowing seeds

Look at the pictures of the crops Aztecs grew in their gardens. Unless you live in a very cold district, you can grow maize (sweetcorn), gourds and pumpkins just like the Aztecs.

1. You can sow the seeds indoors in April or May. Fill some flowerpots with soil or seed compost and put one or two seeds about a centimetre deep in each one.
2. Remember that there was a lake all around the Aztecs' gardens to keep them moist. Keep your pots moist by standing them in saucers and putting some water in the saucers each day.
3. Your seedlings should appear within two weeks. If two come up in a pot, pull one out.
4. At the end of May, you can put your plants in the school garden. (You can also sow seeds outside in May.) Choose a sunny position, and try to put your seeds or plants in a block, not a row.
5. Water the plants in dry weather, especially at first. Your crops should be ready in September.
6. The Aztecs sometimes had to eat food that was not very good for them. Your teacher will tell you whether your crops are good to eat. Perhaps you can dry the maize and grind the seeds into flour for making tortillas. The Aztecs sometimes hollowed out the gourds to make musical instruments.

To be healthy, everyone needs the protein found in certain foods. To get enough protein, rich Aztecs ate turkeys, hairless dogs and fish from the sea. The poor ate little fish and green slime taken from the lake, frogs, snails, insect eggs, maggots and flies pressed together into small cakes.

Aztec crops

Look at **Sources A–D** of four crops the Aztecs grew.

1. Try to identify them.
2. Why do you think the rich and poor got their protein from different foods?

Source A

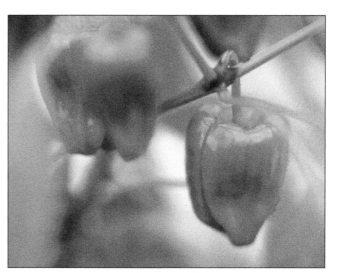

Source C

Source B

Source D

Deerskin pages of an Aztec codex.

The Aztecs did not have books like ours. Instead of paper they used animal skins or the bark from trees. There were 12 stages in making an Aztec book:

1 *The Aztecs shot deer or other animals with bows and arrows.*

2 *They sliced off the skins.*

3 *They stripped bark from trees.*

4 *They soaked the skins to stop them decaying.*

5 *They beat the skins or bark with hammers which made the material soft and smooth.*

6 *They cut it into lengths, which they joined together to make a long roll.*

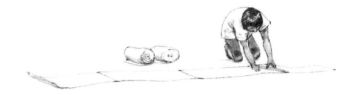

7 *They coated it in white paint.*

8 *They painted the pictures using colours obtained from shells, cacti, beetles, petals, shellfish, soot and oil, chalky stones, leaves, rocks and clay.*

9 *They added black outlines.*

10 *They scratched the roll where they wanted to fold it.*

11 *They folded it backwards and forwards.*

12 *They added covers at each end.*

The feel of a codex

Think about the feel, look and smell of an Aztec book, and the sound and puff of air it would make when you closed it.

Imagine that you are handling one for the first time and write a paragraph describing some of the things you notice.

Making an Aztec book

1. The Aztecs painted their books with brushes. How do you think they made the brushes?
2. They added black outlines with a sort of pen. What do you think the pens were made of?
3. Why do you think the Aztecs scratched the picture roll before they folded it?
4. What do you think the covers of Aztec books were made from?
5. Make your own 'Aztec book'.

Key idea

codex

Our alphabet uses letters to stand for sounds, and the sounds make up words. Aztec writing is made up of lots of little pictures. Some of the pictures have fingers, flags or feathers sticking out of them. These stand for numbers.

= 1

= 20

= 400

Aztec taxes

The pictures show things that other tribes sent to the Aztecs as taxes.

1. Looking at the pictures below, identify the following goods:
   a feathered shield
   a battledress
   beads
   a bunch of feathers
   a bag of beans
   a sack of chilli peppers (marked with a pepper).
2. How many bags of beans were sent?
3. How many bundles of feathers were sent?
4. What do you think the feathers were used for?

The Aztecs sometimes put two or three pictures together to make up the name of a person or place. For example, there was an Aztec city called Quauhtitlan. The name sounded like the Aztec words for tree and teeth (*quauitl* and *tlantli*). To 'spell' this name, the Aztecs painted a tree with some teeth sticking out of it.

 = Quauhtitlan

In a similar way, we could draw an iron bar and a king to stand for the English place-name Barking. We could also draw a ray of light and a mound of soil to stand for the boy's name Raymond. (Ray-mound doesn't sound quite like Raymond, but people would soon get used to it if there wasn't any other way of writing.)

 + = Barking

 +  = Raymond

A new way of writing

Read the place names in the table.

1. Draw one, two or three little pictures to make up each name.
2. Choose a place yourself and write it in the spare box. Ask a friend to draw pictures for it.

Enfield	Dartmouth

Bath	Braintree	Cowes	Gateshead

Hertford	Rugby	Liverpool	

The Aztecs used a special calendar for fortune telling and magic. They gave the days 20 names (like Wind, House, Lizard and Snake) and 13 numbers. Each day had a different name and a different number from the one before. The first day was One Reed, the second day was Two Big Cat and the third was Three Eagle. On the fourteenth day, the number One came round again but the name was a new one – Death's Head or Skull. It was 260 days before One Reed came round again.

The Aztecs carved this stone to show all sorts of things about the days and the stars.

One way to understand the magic calendar is to think of two wheels like the ones in the drawing on page 27. On one wheel there are cocoa beans to stand for the numbers; the other wheel has pictures and names. The first day is One Reed, since the single bean and the reeds are together. Now think what would happen if you turned both wheels a little way: the pair of beans and the Big Cat picture would come together, showing that the second day was Two Big Cat.

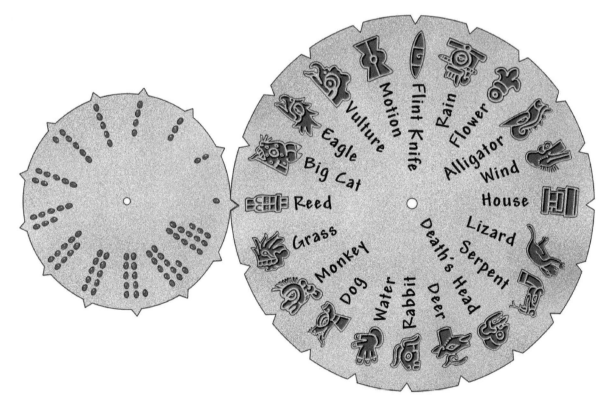

Source A *The Magic Calendar*

A

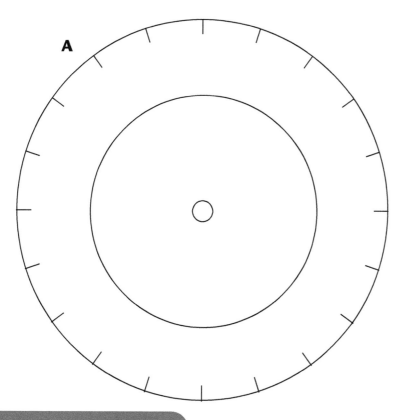

B

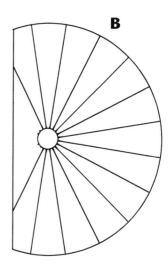

Make a magic calendar (as seen in **Source A**) of your own to understand how the Aztecs knew which day it was.

1. Cut out circle **A** and shape **B** and glue on to card.

2. Around the edge of circle **A**, draw your own pictures for the different days. (Be careful not to draw inside the inner circle.)

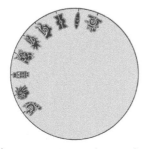

3. Draw the correct numbers of cocoa beans in each space on shape **B**.

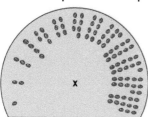

4. Fix **A** and **B** together with a paper fastener.

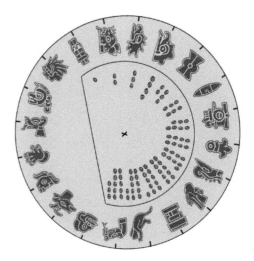

5. Line up the single bean with your reed. You can now see the names of the first 13 days. To find the names of the next 13 days, turn the 'bean wheel' 13 places. The single bean should now be by your picture for day 14.

6. What is the 18th day called?

7. What is the 27th day called?

9 Once in a Lifetime

The number of days in the Aztecs' magical calendar did not match the number of days in a year, so each year had a different starting day, which gave the year its name. It was 52 years before a year with the same name came round again.

The magical calendar started with the day One Reed, so when this was also New Year's Day the Aztecs were very excited and frightened. They wondered whether the sun would rise that particular morning. The gods might decide to end the world or they might give another 52 years of sunlight and life.

There were extra prayers and sacrifices during the night, as the Aztecs begged the gods to allow the day and the year One Reed to begin. This happened only once every 52 years – just once in a lifetime – so people never knew what to expect.

This is how a modern writer describes the night before One Reed of the year Reed:

All fires were put out, even the sacred flames on the temple altars; and all household furniture, ornaments, all the little family gods, were thrown into the lake, the empty houses swept clean, the pregnant women locked up for fear they might be changed into wild beasts, the children forcibly kept awake to save them from being turned into rats.

As the sun finally set, Montezuma climbed to the temple that looks out over all the Valley of Mexico. The end of the world, or the birth of another fifty-two years – which was it to be? The suspense was appalling. Fear ran through the night and the city was silent as the people stared up at the little group on the summit of the old volcano.

The priests had all put on the masks of the gods they served. The dark night wore on. No terrible blaze destroyed the earth. The world did not end.

Suddenly word was passed to the idol room; five priests seized the victim and flung him across the sacrificial stone. A blade slashed open his chest, the heart was plucked out, and in the gaping wound the new fire was kindled by the oldest of methods, a wooden spindle. It was a moment of wild rejoicing. Runners lit their torches from the solitary flame and ran through the starlit night, from village to village. Long before dawn, bonfires blazed the length of the Valley, and every hearth in every home burned with the new-born fire.

(Adapted from *The Conquistadors*, H. Innes, Collins 1986.)

10 Aztec Weaving

The passage below explains how an Aztec girl would have weaved.

She has two wooden rods joined together with many threads. One rod is tied to a post and the other has a band which goes behind her back. She uses her body to keep the threads tight.

The girl has some more thread on a stick. She uses the stick to weave it among the threads in front of her. She weaves under and over, under and over until she has worked her way right across. Then she changes direction and works her way back across the frame. She keeps unwinding the thread as she needs it. After a while she uses a comb to pull the new threads towards herself – she wants to have them close together.

Weaving some cloth

The idea of weaving is simple but weaving well requires skill.

Try to make some cloth of your own. If you use a frame with four sides it will keep the threads tight for you. You could hang your frame from the arm of a chair. Use **Sources A**, **B** and **C** to help you.

Source A

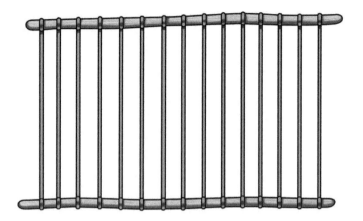

Source B

Source C

Weaving in modern Mexico.

On 12th October, 1492, Columbus reached some islands in Central America. He said that the inhabitants 'were all as naked as the day they were born' and 'wore their hair in a fringe with some long strands at the back'. He also said that he gave them red caps to wear on their heads and beads to wear round their necks.

About 30 years later, Cortés saw the Aztecs wearing beautiful clothes. Perhaps it seems strange that the Aztecs wore clothes when the people on the islands did not. A difference in the weather might give you a clue to one of the reasons. The weather in Mexico was sometimes hotter and sometimes colder than the weather on the islands.

Clothes, hats and jewellery

Read the information on this page. It should give you ideas on the reasons why people wear clothes and other things.

1. The Aztecs wore clothes to keep warm or cool. Why else might they have worn clothes when the people in Central America did not?
2. Discuss the reasons why people wear clothes nowadays.
3. Make a list of things people wear on their heads and give a reason for each. (The pictures in **Source D** will help you.)

Cortés had not yet met the Aztecs who lived in the centre of Mexico but he had heard of them. He asked the natives questions about them. They said that the Aztecs were ruled by a man called Montezuma. They lived in the city of Tenochtitlan, which was built on an island and they made war on the rest of Mexico. Those who gave in peacefully had to pay heavy taxes; those who were beaten in battle were turned into slaves.

The natives did not like Montezuma's taxes but they had to pay them. They did not have money, so payments were always made in goods.

Source A *A mask of an Aztec Sun god.*

Source B
A list of the things one tribe had to send Montezuma in a year. It is a tax list.

> **2400 loads of cloth, cut into large pieces for people to wear**
>
> **800 loads of embroidered cloth, cut into small pieces**
>
> **5 suits made of feathers, to protect chiefs in battle**
>
> **60 suits made from feathers, to protect ordinary warriors in battle**
>
> **40 suits for wearing in battle, with the feathers arranged in a special pattern**
>
> **1 chest of beans**
>
> **5 chests of maize**
>
> **8000 boxes of paper (made from the bark of a tree)**
>
> **2000 loaves of very white salt, for use by the lords of Mexico only**
>
> **8000 lumps of copal (incense) for burning in front of idols**

(Adapted from an unascribed source in *The Conquistadors*, H. Innes, Collins 1986.)

Taxes

The tax list in **Source B** gives us information on what the Aztecs owned, what they ate and what things they thought were valuable. Read the list carefully.

1. What does the list tell you about the Aztecs' lifestyle?

foods	
drink	
clothes	
jewellery	
metals	
activities	
worship	

2. Explain what might have been drunk from the cup in **Source D**.

Artefacts used in worship

Look at the photographs of the pendant and the mask (**Sources A** and **C**).

1. What was used to make each of these?
2. Describe the animal shown in the pendant. What is unusual about it?

Strange substances

Imagine Aztec priests burning incense in front of idols. (Look again at page 13.)

1. Describe what they would see, hear and smell.
2. Find out what copal, amber, cochineal and lime are.
3. What would they have been used for?

400 small baskets of best white copal

100 copper axes

80 loads of ordinary cocoa

800 cups (used for drinking cocoa)

1 little container, made of small turquoise stones

4000 loads of lime

1 load of gold tiles, as thick as a finger

40 bags of cochineal

20 cases of gold dust

1 gold crown

20 lip jewels made of amber and gold

100 pots of liquid amber

8000 handfuls of rich scarlet feathers

40 animal skins

1600 bundles of cotton

Key ideas

gods   worship
taxation

Source D *A cup found in Tenochtitlan.*

33

12 The Spaniards March Inland

The natives said that Montezuma's capital city, Tenochtitlan, was built partly on land and partly on water. The Spaniards were puzzled, but they knew they would soon see the city for themselves. They began to march inland.

Source A *A picture from the time showing the Spaniards marching to Tenochtitlan.*

Tapia described what the march was like:

We left the natives, who had become our friends, and for a hundred kilometres or more we crossed the badlands; there were salt water lakes and we suffered from hunger but more from thirst. At last we reached a town called Zacollan. Cortés asked the lord of this town whether he was ruled by Montezuma, and he replied, 'And who can there be who is not a servant of this great lord?'

(A few days later) Cortés reached an idol house that had two or three little buildings around it, where we put our baggage ... Certain natives came to Cortés, bringing five other natives with them and saying, 'If you are a god that eats meat and blood, eat these men and we shall bring you more. And if you are a kind god, here are feathers and copal. And if you are a man, here are turkeys, maize, bread and cherries.'

(After several days marching) we reached the city of Cholula, and Cortés sent a number of men to explore a smoking volcano we could see. Meanwhile, Montezuma's messengers came to see us in the city. They said that Montezuma would die of fright if we went to see him. They also said that Montezuma had lions and tigers and other wild beasts that he could let loose on us.

Source B *A shield used by the Aztecs during ceremonies and battles.*

Marching to Tenochtitlan

1. Tapia mentions the 'badlands'. What was bad about them?
2. List three things the natives thought Cortés might be. In each case, say what they brought as a present.
3. Describe the Aztec shield in **Source B**. What is it made from? How was it used?
4. What weapons and protection did the Spaniards have?

Key ideas

gods   ruler
invasion   war

Entering the city

Look back at **Source A**, the drawing of Spanish forces marching into Mexico.

1. Try to find some people who might be native Mexicans. What are they doing?
2. Why do you think they are helping the Spaniards?
3. What sign did the Spaniards put on their flag?
4. Why was this sign important to them?
5. Suggest which figure in the drawing might be Cortés. Why do you think so?

Imagining the great Montezuma

As they gathered around their campfires at night, the Spaniards discussed Montezuma and what sort of person he might be.

Imagine you are one of the Spanish soldiers. Make up a conversation between Tapia, Cortés and yourself. For example, you could start with Cortés saying: cunning, cowardly or powerful.

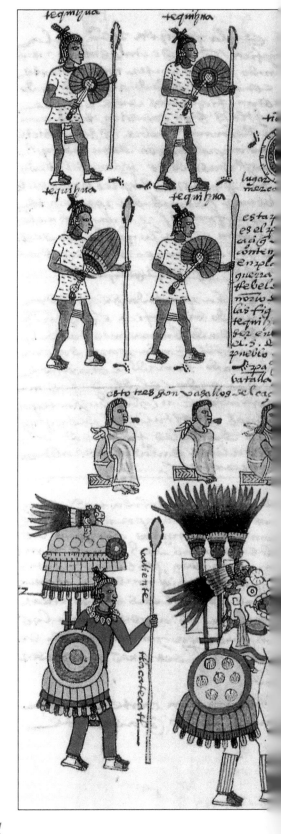

Native armies fought several battles against the Spaniards and one of the fiercest took place near Cholula. A Spaniard called Gomara described the battle (which the Spaniards won) and the natives' weapons and battledress:

The men were armed in their finest way. Their faces were painted with red dye, and they looked like devils. They carried plumes and moved about on the battlefield with amazing skill. Their weapons were slings, pikes, lances and swords; bows and arrows. They had helmets on their heads and wooden armour on their arms and legs. Their large and small shields, which were very fine and not at all weak, were of tough wood and leather, with brass and feather ornaments. Their wooden swords had flint set into them, which cut well and made a nasty wound. They fought in large groups, each with many trumpets, conches and drums, all of which were a sight to see.

36

This Aztec page tells us about their weapons. A Spaniard has written the notes on it.

Source C *Aztec shield, arrows and helmet.*

Warriors

Read the passage written by Gomara.

1. What does Gomara think of the natives' armour? What details seem to impress him most?
2. Why do you think the native soldiers painted their faces?
3. List the materials which Gomara mentions.
4. Look at **Source C**. Describe the Aztecs' weapons and armour.
5. A conch is a natural object. Find out what it is and what it is used for.
6. Why do you think the Spaniards won the battle?

Key ideas

symbols of christianity
war

Source A *The city of Tenochtitlan, built on a huge lake.*

The Spaniards were soon in the Aztecs' part of Mexico. At last they reached a lake that had formed in the crater of an old volcano. Roads built on soil led across the lake, and there in the centre the Spaniards could see the gleaming city of Tenochtitlan.

The Spaniards left us detailed descriptions of Tenochtitlan. One of them wrote:

This great city is built in the salty part of a lake. It is joined to the land by three high roads built of stone and earth. Along one of these roads a canal has been built, bringing good fresh water from a mountain stream.

As the Spaniards marched into Tenochtitlan there were two lines of Aztec nobles coming to meet them.

According to a Spaniard called Aguilar:

Between them came the great King Montezuma, in a curtained throne. He could be seen by no one, and none of the Aztecs dared stare at the throne, which they carried on their shoulders. In front of Montezuma walked a man with a long mace in his hand, representing Montezuma's greatness.

When Cortés was within a stone's throw of Montezuma he got off his horse. Montezuma then appeared and placed necklaces of gold and precious stones about Cortés, and Cortés placed a string of painted beads about Montezuma's neck.

Key ideas

capital city   civilisation

Montezuma swore in front of a scribe to obey and serve His Majesty Charles V of Spain. He said that word had been handed down from his ancestors that bearded and armed men were to come from where the sun rises and they were not to be attacked.

Tenochtitlan

1. Look at **Source A**. Why do you think the Aztecs built Tenochtitlan on a lake? Describe the land that surrounded the lake.
2. How can you tell that Montezuma was a very important ruler?
3. Why did Montezuma welcome the Spaniards?
4. Describe the gifts exchanged between Cortés and Montezuma. The text and **Source B**, the picture of the meeting, will help.
5. Explain how the Spaniards came 'from where the sun rises'.

Source B *A picture from the time showing Cortés' meeting with Montezuma.*

The Aztecs made necklaces similar to the two on these pages using gold and precious stones.

Use all the information and pictures in this chapter.

1. Whose gifts were worth more – the gifts Montezuma gave Cortés or the gifts Cortés gave Montezuma?
2. What might have been the reason for this?
3. What were the Aztecs' attitudes to Cortés? List four or five things in the passage which make this clear.
4. Copy the table and tick the box next to any statements you agree with.

Montezuma's headdress

According to Cortés, Montezuma said this:

You have come from where the sun rises. From this, and from what you tell us of your great lord or king who has sent you here, we firmly believe that he is our rightful sovereign (ruler).

According to an Aztec, Montezuma said this:

I have met you face to face! I was in agony for five days, for ten days, with my eyes fixed on the Region of the Mystery. And now you have come out of the clouds and mists to sit on your throne again. You have come back to us; you have come down from the sky.

Entering Tenochtitlan

Montezuma thinks the Spaniards are gods.	
Cortés is going to rule the Aztecs himself.	
Montezuma accepts the Emperor (Charles V) as his ruler.	
There was a scribe to take notes.	

5. What precious metals did the Aztecs have? How do you know?
6. How would Montezuma have felt wearing his headdress?

Key ideas

gods   sovereign

Different opinions

There are three accounts in this chapter of the first meeting between Montezuma and Cortés.

1. Are there any differences between the three?
2. Discuss why people give different accounts of the same event. You could start by comparing what you and your friends say about something that has happened in your school or town. You could also compare reports in newspapers.
3. According to an Aztec, Montezuma spent five or ten days in agony with his eyes 'fixed on the Region of the Mystery'. Discuss the meaning of this with your friends.

Holy Places in Tenochtitlan

Skull racks displayed enemy warriors' heads.

The Spaniards were amazed when they entered the square in the centre of Montezuma's city.

According to Tapia:

There would have been space for 400 Spaniards to build their houses. (The square had) a huge stone platform with 113 steps (leading up it). On the top were two towers, and in one of these was the Aztecs' main god. He was made from all kinds of seeds, which had been ground and mixed up with boys' and girls' blood, making a shape which was fatter than a man and just as tall. On feast days they put gold jewellery ... and very fine clothes on the figure.

There was also a second platform with towers, but Tapia does not say how high it was. Perhaps he forgot because he was so surprised to see thousands of skulls staring from it. Between the towers there were 60 or 70 tall wooden posts, and from top to bottom they were linked together with wooden rods. This made a rack for the skulls. The Aztecs had bored two holes in each skull, and they had pushed five skulls on to every rod. Tapia and another Spaniard worked out that there were 136 000 skulls altogether.

Key ideas

idol   sacrifice

Tapia wondered where all the skulls might have come from, and he asked Montezuma why he and his captains did not wipe out a troublesome tribe. Montezuma replied:

We could easily do so. But then we would have nowhere to train our youths except in far away places. Also, we wish to have people at hand to sacrifice to our gods.

Source D *The 'Eagle Knight' warrior was dedicated to the Sun god. He is shown on this knife.*

Source C *An Aztec drawing of a sacrifice to the Sun god.*

A sacrifice

Look at **Source C**, the picture showing an Aztec priest and two victims.

1. Which is the priest and which are the victims?
2. What is the priest doing?
3. What is the man on the steps doing?
4. The idol in one of the towers was the Aztecs' god of rain. Why do you think this god was important?
5. Find the heart and say why you think the artist drew it in the air.
6. The artist was an Aztec himself, and he drew his picture shortly after the Spaniards had taken his country over. Do you think he was likely to give a good picture of Aztec life? Why?
7. According to Tapia, the statue of the god was made from certain things. What were they and why do you think they were chosen?
8. Look at **Source D**. What was the knife with the 'Eagle Knight' warrior decoration used for?

Archaeologists are people who study things that remain from the past. They have many questions about the Aztecs' towers or temples. Did each tribe have its own sort of tower – or several sorts? Did styles of building change with time? Did people pass on old ideas and change them accidentally?

Clay models of the temples survive today, giving us clues about their appearance.

Key ideas

archaeologist   temple
evidence

Only one Aztec temple still survives in Mexico. Bodies were sacrificed on the platform and rolled down the steps to soften the flesh for eating.

Were writers and artists sometimes careless about what they said or showed in their work? Did writers and artists sometimes exaggerate or try to mislead others?

Archaeologists now know a lot about the temples in Mexico, even though most have fallen down or been destroyed. Clues have come from the places where temples stood, pictures of the temples, models made for people to keep in their homes and Spanish descriptions of the temples.

A Spaniard called Juan Díaz landed on the Mexican coast and described an idol room 'eight spans wide and the height of a man'. He did not mention any platform. Tapia said that the towers in Tenochtitlan were higher than a pike and a half and stood on huge platforms.

The trouble with having all these clues is that sometimes they seem to disagree.

Aztec temple decoration.

Investigating historical evidence

Look at all the information in this chapter that tells you (or shows you) what Aztec temples were like.

1. The clues give different ideas about what the towers were like. What are the most important differences?
2. Discuss why the clues differ in what they tell us about the towers.
3. Do you think the towers at Tenochtitlan were round or square? You will have to decide which clues can be trusted and which cannot.

Measuring and comparing

Think about what you have read in this chapter.

1. Why do you think the Spaniards talked about pikes and spans instead of using measurements like metres?
2. How did people use their bodies to measure things before they had rulers?
3. Who do you think destroyed the temples? Why?
4. What do we call people who dig up and study clues from the past?

To make the tower or idol room

1. Cut out the shape on page 47 and glue it onto card.
2. Score along the dotted lines.
3. Fold the card where you have scored and glue the tabs to the opposite sides to make a box. This will be your idol room.
4. Make a base for your tower. If you make a wide base you and a friend can both fix your towers to it. Then you will have a double temple like the one at Tenochtitlan.

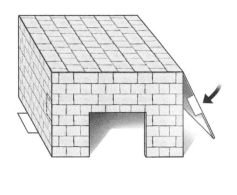

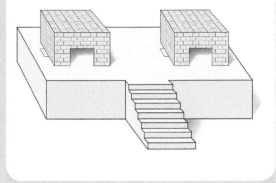

Pleasing the gods

1. Decide what you will add to your temple. You might want to make a skull rack or have a place to burn fires all night. Maybe you will decorate your temple or build another room where soldiers or animals will keep guard.
2. Decide how to finish the temple. Perhaps you can use some of the following materials: thread, beads, crayons, silver paper, egg boxes, string, yogurt pots, paint, twigs, straw, stones, sugar paper, felt, tape, glue, water, card, milk bottle tops, mud, flowers.

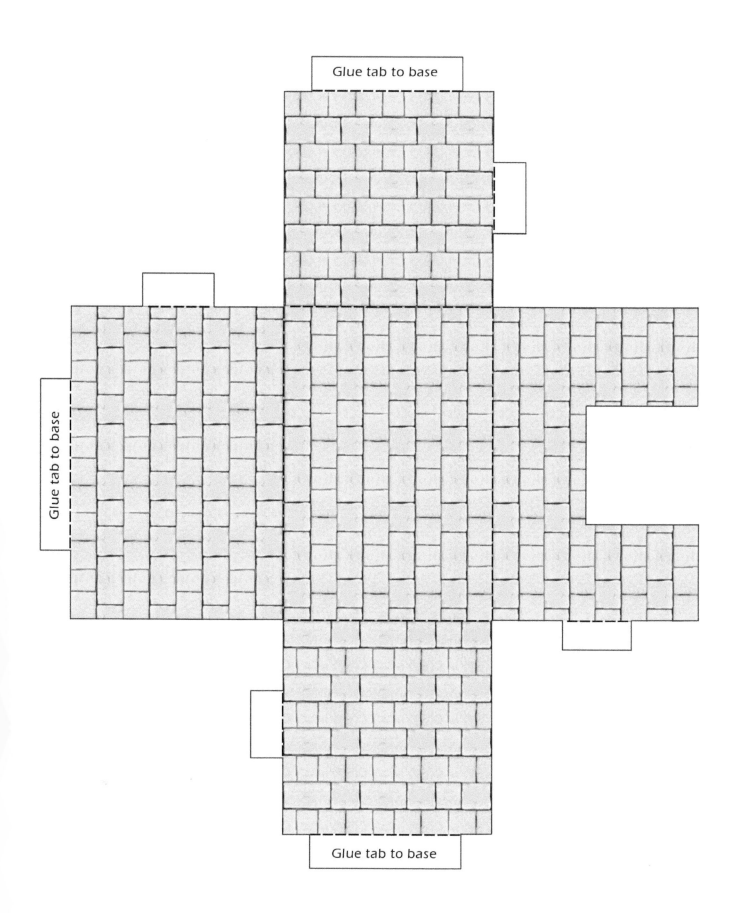

Glue tab to base

Glue tab to base

Glue tab to base

15 Fine Houses

The Spaniards were amazed when they saw Tenochtitlan.

This is what a Spaniard wrote about the streets and houses:

The streets are wide and beautiful. Two or three of the main ones are built on an island but the rest are half water and half banks of soil. The people walk on the soil or ride canoes on the water. The canoes are dug out of tree trunks, and some are large enough to hold five people easily.

There are other streets which are all water, so people have to go by canoe. Without their canoes they would not be able to get to their houses.

The houses belonging to the lords were so large and had so many rooms that they were amazing to see.

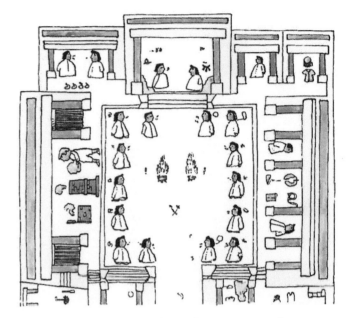

Source A *A plan of an Aztec palace.*

Key ideas

court   palace
fortress   ruler
gradeur

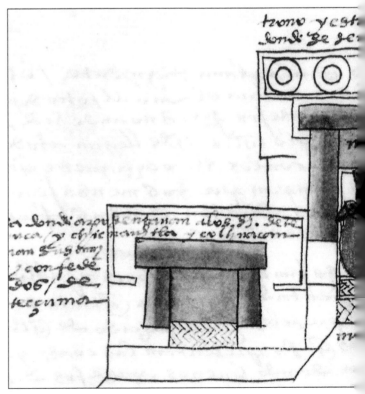

Source B *Montezuma in his palace. A Spaniard has written notes on the picture.*

Montezuma's palace

Look at **Sources A** and **B**.

1. Do you think the palaces were built of wood or stone? What clues help you?
2. Find the room where a king and his son are.
3. Find the central courtyard. What are the people doing there?
4. Which source do you think gives a better idea of the size of Montezuma's palace?
5. Explain why Montezuma kept people as well as animals in his collection.

According to a Spaniard:

At one of his houses Montezuma kept cages of wolves, foxes, lions, tigers and other wild cats. There were also cages with birds of prey such as falcons and hawks. It amazed me to see how much meat they ate and how many people there were to look after them. From large clay jars came the rattling sound of snakes and vipers, helping to show Montezuma's importance, and he kept men and women who were crippled, deformed or had not grown properly.

He also kept every possible kind of water bird. I can swear that more than 600 men spent all their time looking after them. There was even a special place for sick birds. With the water birds Montezuma kept people whose eyebrows, hair and bodies were completely white.

Another Spaniard described the lords' houses like this:

It was the custom in all the lords' houses to have very large rooms and halls around a courtyard, and in one of the houses there was a hall large enough to hold more than 3000 people comfortably. And the house was also so large that 30 men could have had a mock battle on the roof as if they were on a great square.

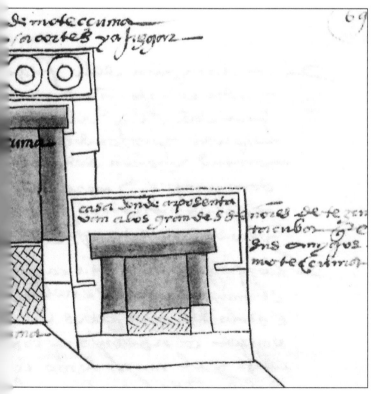

City homes

Read the descriptions of the houses in Tenochtitlan.

1. Do you think all the houses were built on wooden posts?
2. Did the houses in Tenochtitlan have flat or sloping roofs? Why?
3. Do you think the temple in Tenochtitlan was built on land or over water? Explain your answer.

16 Aztec Children

There were schools in Tenochtitlan but village children stayed at home and learnt by helping their parents. By reading and looking carefully at these pages, you can find out how parents treated children who misbehaved.

Life as a child

Source B shows how Aztec parents treated their children. The number of dots tells us the age of the children, and you can see how many tortillas (small pancakes) they were given each day.

1. Study the pictures and discuss them with friends.
2. Try to fill in the table opposite. The small boxes just need numbers. In the big boxes you should say what you think the picture shows. To help you here are two of the answers:
   The father is punishing the boy by holding him over a bonfire.
   The girl is learning to grind maize.

Playing or fighting

Look at **Source A**.

Does it show children playing or men fighting? There is plenty to discuss!

Source A

	Pictures on the left		Pictures on the right
1st row	Age:	Tortillas each day:	Tortillas each day:
2nd row	Age:	Tortillas each day:	Tortillas each day:
3rd row	Age:	Tortillas each day:	Tortillas each day:
4th row	Age:	Tortillas each day:	Tortillas each day:

Source B

Source A *This ball court can still be seen in Mexico.*

The Aztecs played all sorts of games. One, which the Spaniards called volador (flying), was very risky. The Aztecs took the trunk of a tall, straight tree and fixed it up in a village or town. They coiled four lengths of rope round the top and built a platform a little way down. The platform could spin round and round.

At the chosen time, four men dressed as birds climbed up to the platform. Someone tied the ropes round their waists and they jumped off. As soon as they did so, the ropes began to unwind from the post. The platform started going round and the men circled downwards, towards the ground. After 13 circles, they finally skidded to a halt in the dust and everyone cheered.

The Aztecs also used poles and ropes in another way. They scrambled up them to reach and eat a sugary figure at the top. The figure was probably made to look like one of their gods.

Volador

Look at **Source B**.

1. Explain why parts of the branches were left on the volador pole.
2. The Aztecs thought about their gods when they watched volador. Try to decide why.
3. Pretend that you are one of the volador 'bird men' and write about what it was like to take part. Remember the dangers.

Source B *Volador 'gods'.*

Young men from rich families played a game called tlachtli. This was played on a court as big as a modern football pitch, with walls three times as high as the players. Fixed in the middle of each wall there was a stone ring. It was too high to reach, but the players had to knock a rubber ball through it using only their elbows, knees or thighs.

The game was fast and furious. The players were in two teams and they competed fiercely, diving for the ball on the hard stone floor. People watched excitedly from the tops of the walls, often betting on which team would win. If anyone scored, the players were allowed to rob the spectators, who would try to run away.

Trying to score at tlachtli.

A game of patolli.

The Aztecs also played a board game called patolli. It was rather like ludo, but with beans as dice and counters. To bring themselves luck, they spoke to the beans, rubbed them between their hands and burned incense. Some Aztecs would bet so much on patolli and other games that they got into debt and had to sell themselves as slaves.

Tlachtli

Read the description of tlachtli.

1. Do you think it was easy or hard to score?
2. How does the tlachtli court in **Source A** differ from the court described in the text? Suggest a possible reason for the difference.

Patolli

1. Make a patolli board by drawing it on paper or chalking it on the ground.
2. With friends, try to play the game.
3. Write down the rules.

Key ideas

entertainment   slavery

Source A *Battle in the city. An Aztec drew this picture many years after the battle.*

Cortés and the Spaniards had taken control of Tenochtitlan, but they acted in a very peaceful manner. They treated Montezuma well and they let him stay in one of his palaces.

Things went wrong when Cortés and most of his men left the city. A small group of Spaniards stayed behind and one day they attacked the Aztecs' leaders and priests in the city's holy square. The people of Tenochtitlan turned on the Spaniards, and Cortés had to hurry back to deal with the fighting. Montezuma was killed but the Tenochtitlans finally drove the Spaniards out of the city. All the Spaniards could do was surround the lake and cut off the city's water supply. The Aztecs had to drink rainwater and eat the food they could grow for themselves.

A Spaniard called Bernal Díaz described what the Spaniards found when they entered the silent city a few weeks later:

The houses were full of dead bodies, and there were some poor Mexicans still alive who were too weak to move. The city looked as if it had been ploughed up. Even the roots of plants had been dug out, boiled and eaten, and they had even eaten the bark of some trees.

Key ideas

conquering   ruler
invasion   war

Remembering the attack

Work in groups of three. One of you should pretend to be a Spanish soldier and one should pretend to be an Aztec whose family has starved to death in Tenochtitlan. The third person is to hold a radio or television interview. They should ask questions to find out what both feel about the following:

1. The attack on the holy square.
2. The way people starved to death.
3. The fact that the Spaniards are building a new city (Mexico City) where Tenochtitlan stood.

Attack on the holy square

Look at **Source A**, which shows the Spaniards invading the holy square.

1. Who are the figures at the top of the tower?
2. Do you think the men playing musical instruments are Spaniards or Aztecs? Why do you think so?
3. What sort of instruments are they playing? How are they playing them?
4. Do you think the man with the flag is a Spaniard or an Aztec? How can you tell?
5. Which side seems to be winning the battle? Why do you think so?
6. Why do you think the Spaniards attacked the Aztecs?
7. What is the artist trying to say about the battle?

A gong from Tenochtitlan.

Source A *A Mexican farmer's home. Aztec farmers built their homes in the same way.*

Aztec houses did not have very much furniture, but they had wooden chests for clothes and other possessions. Both the rich and the poor sat and slept on reed mats. Rich people's homes were full of fine ornaments. Poor people's homes were cluttered with the things that they used every day.

Tenochtitlan had been destroyed, but many Aztecs still lived in villages around the lake. Their homes were built on dry land and were simpler and smaller than those in the city. There was just one room with an earthen floor.

When an Aztec wanted to build a new house he began by knocking posts into the ground. The posts made a framework for the finished house. The Aztec fixed twigs between the posts and then plastered them with sticky clay. The sun baked the clay, which kept rain and draughts out. The house was probably snug but gloomy, with no windows and just a large doorway.

The Aztec finished the house with a sloping, thatched roof. Thatch was good because it was made of lots of separate stalks. Smoke from the family's cooking fire could escape between them, but rain was kept out. It would run down the stalks to the edge of the roof and fall to the ground.

A modern author lists things found in an Aztec house:

... broom, the husband's digging stick, seed basket, tools, hunting or fishing gear, the wife's loom, her water jar, cooking and storage pots, a vessel containing maize kernels soaking in lime water, and the stone on which she ground the maize.

Each household owned one or more images of the gods, made in wood, stone or baked clay. In some homes, a cage containing a talking parrot or a song-bird hung on the wall.

Figures of the gods and ornaments from Aztec homes.

Key ideas

gods   idol

Village home

Imagine you are an Aztec who is about to build a new home.

1. Draw and describe how you would do this.
2. List the materials you would need.

Family life

Read the information on Aztec houses built outside the city, and look at **Source A**.

1. How could villagers stop draughts blowing in through their doorways?
2. How could they give themselves light in the evenings?
3. Using the list of family possessions, say which jobs were done by men and which were done by women.

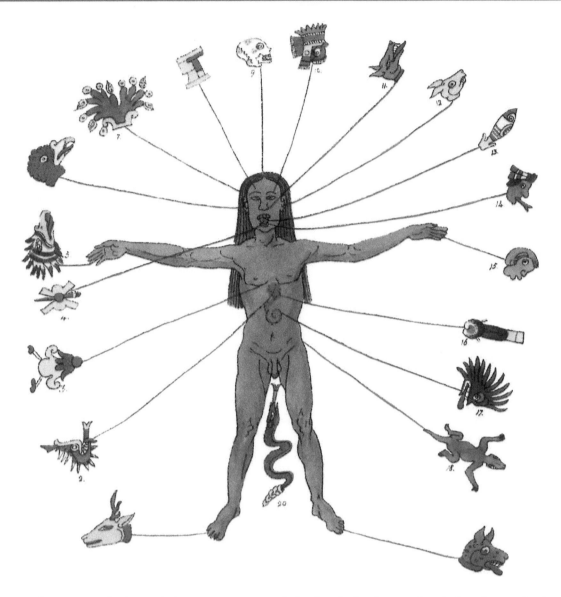

Source A *The Aztecs believed that every part of the body had an animal that brought it good or bad luck and health.*

When the Aztecs were ill they blamed evil spells, or they thought that the gods were punishing them for doing wrong. They visited healers, who tried to decide what was causing the illness and how to cure it. Often the healer said prayers or spells, and she would use medicines made from plants.

There were hundreds of these herbal medicines, and many of them worked very well.

The Spaniards gave the Aztecs diseases like measles and smallpox, which they had never had before.

Bernal Díaz tells us about a Spaniard called Narvaez, who sailed to Mexico in 1520:

One of the men Narvaez brought with him had smallpox; it was sad that this disease entered the country, for it spread with unbelievable speed, killing thousands of Aztecs; not knowing what it was they threw themselves into cold water to deal with the fever and this caused their death.

Soon the Aztecs were quarrelling over who should take over plots of land and the important jobs. Cortés sometimes settled these quarrels by giving the land or the jobs to the Spaniards.

A plague over Mexico

According to a 19th century writer, William Prescott, smallpox swept over Mexico 'like fire over the prairies'. The Aztecs died 'in heaps like cattle', but the Spaniards survived.

Suggest two or three possible reasons for this. Use clues in this chapter and talk about it with your friends.

Source B *A healer treating a patient. (The round things are the Aztecs' way of showing his daily ration of bread.)*

The fight for land and jobs

Think carefully about what has been explained in this chapter.

1. Why do you think there were suddenly lots of quarrels over land and jobs?
2. What did Cortés do?

Key ideas

medicine   plague

Disease and medicine

Look at **Sources A** and **B** and read the passage written by Díaz.

1. Which animal did the Aztecs think helped to cure earache?
2. Which part of the body was helped by a fish?
3. How did smallpox reach Mexico?
4. How did the Aztecs treat the fever that smallpox gave them?
5. What effect did the treatment have?
6. Look at the numbered objects in **Source B**. What might they be?

21 New Crops, New Ideas

Diseases were not the only things that the Spaniards took to the New World. They also took boat-loads of cattle, sheep and pigs. Soon they were rearing them on their new farms, using native American people as slaves.

The Europeans found that sugar cane grew extremely well on their new farms. Today, sugar is still an important crop in Central America.

Some plants which grew in the New World were unknown in Spain and the rest of Europe. These included important crops like maize, tobacco and new sorts of beans. The Spanish settlers began to grow them, and so did many farmers in Europe.

Source A

New crops

Look at **Source A** showing foods made from crops discovered in the New World. The crops are still grown there, and most are now grown in Europe as well.

Name the crops and at least one thing that is made from each.

A modern photograph of sugar cane in flower.

The following passage describes an attack which Spanish soldiers made on some Aztecs. It gives a clue to the reason why the Aztecs did not make vehicles.

The 'stags' approached with the soldiers on their backs. The soldiers were wearing cotton armour. They bore their leather shields and their iron spears in their hands, but their swords hung down from the necks of the 'stags'. These animals wear little bells - they are covered in bells. When the 'stags' gallop, the bells make a din, ringing and clattering. These 'stags', these horses, snort and bellow, and the sweat pours off their bodies in streams. The foam from their mouths drops on to the ground. It spills out in blobs, like the lather from soap plants.

These 'stags' make a terrible noise when they run, they make a great din as though stones were raining on to the earth. Behind them they leave the ground pitted and scarred.

Key ideas

communication   transport
settler

Unfamiliar animals

Read the description of a Spanish attack on the Aztecs.

1. Who wrote this passage – a Spaniard or an Aztec?
2. What does the writer mean by 'stags'? Why does he call the animals 'stags'?
3. List all the noises described in the passage.
4. What do you think the bells were for?
5. Why does the writer give so much detail about the animals?

Perhaps you can already guess why the Aztecs did not have vehicles. If you need more help, think about Aztec merchants and messengers who had to go everywhere on foot. The messengers used tracks from Tenochtitlan to the coast to carry picture letters from Montezuma to the village chiefs. Often they had to run for hours, trying to get to the village before the sun went down. Montezuma demanded fresh sea fish at his table each day and people had to carry the fish from the coast to the city on their backs. Spaniards on horseback frightened them, but they wished that they had horses too.

Fish were caught daily for Montezuma.

Messengers and merchants

Read the information on this page.

1. What sort of things do you think were in Montezuma's letters?
2. Why did the messengers run instead of riding horses?
3. Why did merchants and slaves carry goods instead of using carts?

As well as horses, the Spaniards brought guns and gunpowder with them. These frightened the Aztecs even more than the horses did. The Aztecs did not understand how these new weapons worked. The Spaniards aimed things that looked like sticks or huge tubes. Then, with a bang, there was blood and damage everywhere.

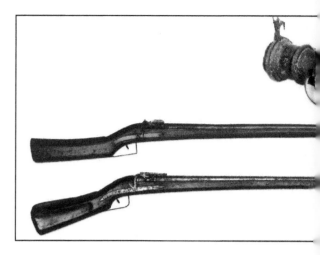

Dangerous sticks

Pretend that you are the Aztec who wrote about the Spanish horses.

Describe what it was like to have your village shot at by Spanish guns and cannons. (Remember – things are always much worse when you do not understand what is happening to you.)

Printing machines were probably just as important as weapons in helping the Spaniards to conquer the Aztecs.

The Aztecs had no idea how to write or print books. They could not use books to spread their ideas and the sea cut them off from new ideas that were spreading throughout Europe.

In the past, Europeans had been like the Aztecs – they had relied on ideas passed from father to son. There were handwritten books, but these were very scarce indeed. It was during the 15th century, shortly before Columbus' time, that they started to use printing machines. Printed books were scarce at first, but their numbers grew quickly. There were books on expeditions to new countries, and books which told of the latest discoveries.

The knowledge collected in printed books helped the Spaniards to reach Mexico and conquer the Aztecs.

Source B *One of the earliest printing presses.* ▼

▲ European guns and cannons similar to those used by the Spaniards to conquer the Americas. How would the men have moved the cannons?

The Spaniards wrote about their adventures and these accounts were often turned into new printed books. One Spanish book describes a law which the Spaniards forced the natives in Mexico to obey:

The natives shall not sing their solemn hymns without having them checked by Christian priests or others who understand their language. The priests shall see that there is nothing unsuitable in the hymns.

Printing

Study the law for the natives.

1. Why do you think Spanish priests and rulers were keen to learn the Aztecs' language?
2. What might the priests have thought 'unsuitable' in the Mexicans' hymns?
3. Look at **Source B**, the picture of the printing press. Explain what each person is doing.
4. How did the invention of printing help the Spaniards?

The natives' way of life was not completely forgotten. As we have seen, some Spaniards described it in their books and others studied the Aztec pictures. Nowadays, archaeologists dig up things that tell us more about the Aztecs and Spaniards.

Key ideas

communication   conversion
conquering

Index